SPIDERS SET II

RECLUSE SPIDERS

Jill C. Wheeler
ABDO Publishing Company

visit us at
www.abdopub.com

Published by ABDO Publishing Company, 4940 Viking Drive, Edina, Minnesota 55435.
Copyright © 2006 by Abdo Consulting Group, Inc. International copyrights reserved in all
countries. No part of this book may be reproduced in any form without written permission from
the publisher. The Checkerboard Library™ is a trademark and logo of ABDO Publishing
Company.

Printed in the United States.

Cover Photo: Animals Animals
Interior Photos: Animals Animals pp. 7, 15, 17, 21; Corbis pp. 5, 18, 19; Index Stock p. 9;
    Peter Arnold p. 13; Visuals Unlimited p. 11

Series Coordinator: Stephanie Hedlund
Editors: Stephanie Hedlund, Megan Murphy
Art Direction: Neil Klinepier

Library of Congress Cataloging-in-Publication Data

Wheeler, Jill C., 1964-
    Recluse spiders / Jill C. Wheeler.
        p. cm. -- (Spiders. Set II)
    Includes bibliographical references.
    ISBN 1-59679-296-5
    1. Loxosceles--Juvenile literature. I. Title.

QL458.42.L6W49 2006
595.4'4--dc22

                                                        2005045277

CONTENTS

RECLUSE SPIDERS

Worldwide, there are 34,000 species of spiders. All spiders are **arachnids**. So are scorpions, ticks, and mites. Arachnids are **arthropods**, too. That means they have a skeleton on the outside of their body.

There is a **family** of arachnids called Loxoscelidae, or recluse spiders. Scientists have found 56 different species in this family. Fifty-four species are found in North, Central, and South America. One lives in the Mediterranean region and another lives in South Africa.

The brown recluse is the most well-known recluse spider. Brown recluses are native to the United States. They can be found from the Midwest to the Gulf of Mexico. Other species of recluse spiders are found in Arizona, California, and New Mexico.

The brown recluse is one member of the Loxoscelidae family. Other species include the desert recluse and the Arizona recluse.

SIZES

Recluse spiders are medium-sized spiders. The leg span of an adult brown recluse is about the size of a quarter. Their bodies are about 12/32 of an inch (10 mm) long and about 6/32 of an inch (5 mm) wide. Males have slightly shorter bodies but longer legs than females.

Brown recluse spiders are not very big. Yet their bites can cause big problems for humans. Some people are unaffected by bites. Others get large, deep, painful wounds from them. The wounds can take months to heal and may leave bad scars.

As recluse spiders grow, they molt several times. This means they shed their outer skeleton. Recluse spiders become adults in about a year. They usually live between two and four years. But, some recluse spiders have lived seven years in laboratories!

Many people are not aware that they have been bitten by a brown recluse spider. They discover the bite when the spider's venom begins to kill the tissue around the area.

SHAPES

Like all spiders, recluse spiders have a front body part called a **cephalothorax**. On top of the recluse spider's cephalothorax is a violin-shaped marking. This is why some people call recluse spiders fiddleback or violin spiders.

Recluse spiders have other body parts common to all spiders. They have eight thin legs attached to their cephalothorax. They also have two **pedipalps** and two **chelicerae**.

All spiders have a wide, rear body part called an abdomen. A recluse's abdomen is round and plump. At the end of the abdomen, these spiders have **spinnerets**. These fingerlike objects are used to spin silk. Spinnerets cannot be seen on some spiders, including recluse spiders.

Most spiders have eight eyes in two rows of four. However, recluse spiders only have six eyes. And, these eyes are arranged in pairs that form a semicircle.

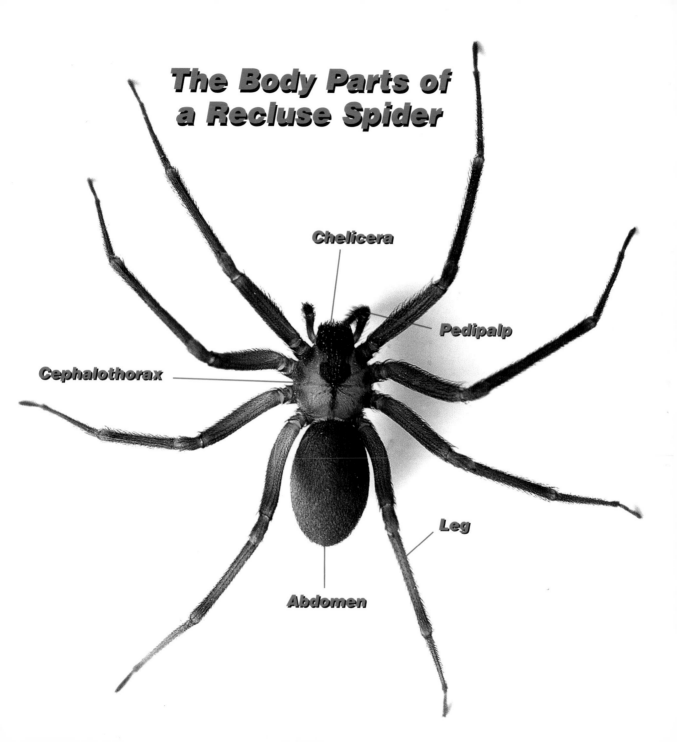

The Body Parts of a Recluse Spider

Chelicera

Pedipalp

Cephalothorax

Abdomen

Leg

COLORS

Recluse spiders range in color from cream to dark brown. Their entire body is the same color. However, their abdomen may be a shade lighter or darker depending on their last meal. Their legs are solid colored with no stripes.

The recluse spider's violin marking is a little darker than the rest of its body. But, this marking can fade as the spider gets older. Sometimes it cannot be seen at all. This depends on the species or when the spider last molted.

The body parts and legs of the recluse spider are covered with very fine hairs. These hairs give the spider a velvety look.

Recluse spiders use their brownish coloring to hide from **predators**. A recluse is someone who likes to stay away from others. Recluse spiders love to hide, so that is how they got their name.

The abdomen of most spiders expands to allow more food to be eaten. This is why a recluse spider's abdomen may be a lighter color after it has had a meal.

WHERE THEY LIVE

Recluse spiders are found in North, Central, and South America. They are also found in South Africa and near the Mediterranean Sea. In these places, recluse spiders may live outdoors or inside buildings.

Recluse spiders are **nocturnal**, and they do not build webs to capture prey. Instead, they wander at night to find food. Before daylight, they find a place to build their loose, messy **retreats** of sticky silk.

Outdoors, recluse retreats may be found under rocks or debris. Indoors, the spiders may hide in attics, basements, or closets. They are also found in toy boxes, shoes, and furniture.

Houses with recluse spiders usually have a lot of them. Researchers found 150 brown recluse spiders in one house in Kansas. In Chile, researchers found recluse spiders in 645 of 2,189 homes searched. The houses with spiders averaged 163 spiders each.

Recluse spiders prefer to spend their time in dark, undisturbed places unless they are hunting.

Senses

Recluse spiders are most active at night. So, their six large eyes let in a lot of light. Yet they do not see very well. In fact, few spider species see well. They rely on their sense of touch instead.

Like all spiders, recluses have fine hairs covering their bodies and legs. These hairs do more than give the recluse a velvety look. They act as sensitive receptors. These receptors pick up and transmit vibrations.

Spiders use vibrations to "listen" to the world around them. The spiders pick up vibrations transmitted through the air, the ground, or their webs. This lets the spiders know what is going on around them. The vibrations also help the spiders avoid **predators** or find prey.

Opposite page: *The hair on the recluse spider's pedipalps helps it sense its surroundings. The hair is even used to sense smells.*

DEFENSE

The recluse spider's **predators** include some insects, birds, and small animals. But, humans can also be a threat. Many people are frightened of recluse spiders. This is especially true of brown recluse spiders because most people know this species is poisonous.

People may kill a spider because they think it might be a brown recluse. Often, it is a different kind of spider. Only a trained scientist can identify a brown recluse by looking at it.

Recluse spiders usually defend themselves by hiding. That is one reason they love to live in people's homes, barns, and sheds. But, they also have a second line of defense.

Recluse spiders will bite an enemy and **inject** it with their powerful **venom**. However, they only bite when they feel threatened. So, most bites happen when someone unknowingly bothers a recluse spider.

Spiders move the first
and third leg on one side at
the same time as they move
the second and fourth on the other.
This helps recluses quickly run from
predators and catch food.

FOOD

Recluse spiders like to eat insects. They like firebrats, crickets, and cockroaches. People with cockroach problems would be lucky to have a few recluse spiders sharing their home.

A firebrat is a wingless insect and a favorite food of recluses.

Recluse spiders leave their **retreats** at night and search for their favorite foods. But, they don't have to eat every night. Recluse spiders can go for months without a meal. Researchers have seen brown recluse spiders go six months without either food or water.

Most spiders eat live prey. Like recluses, most **inject** their prey with **venom** to keep it still. Then, **digestive** juices turn the prey's insides to mush so the spider can suck them out.

Recently, scientists have learned that brown recluses will eat dead bugs. In fact, some scientists believe they prefer them. A group of researchers put brown recluses in a cage with both a live and a dead bug. Eighty percent of the time, the spiders ate the dead one first.

Like this six-spotted fishing spider and all spiders, recluses use a sucking stomach to eat. Their stomach has muscles around it that expand and contract, which make it act as a pump.

Babies

After mating, female recluse spiders lay about 30 to 90 eggs. They encase their eggs in an off-white, silken sac. This sac is about 21/32 of an inch (17 mm) across. A female may create several egg sacs over the course of several months.

Baby spiders, or spiderlings, emerge from the egg sac in about a month. They grow slowly, especially if it is cold or if they do not have much to eat.

Spiderlings molt several times during their first year. The spiderlings quickly grow new skeletons. Recluse spiderlings reach maturity in 10 to 12 months.

Recluse spiders never go far from where they are born. Other species of spiders **migrate** by **ballooning**. However, recluse spiders have to get a hand from humans if they want to travel. Recluse spiders have been found in many strange areas after hitching a ride.

All spiders molt as they grow. This Mexican red-kneed tarantula is leaving behind its skeleton.

GLOSSARY

arachnid (uh-RAK-nuhd) - an order of animals with two body parts and eight legs.

arthropod - a member of the phylum Arthropoda with an exterior skeleton.

balloon - to use a strand of silk to ride the air current to a new location. Some spiderlings balloon to migrate.

cephalothorax (seh-fuh-luh-THAWR-aks) - the front body part of an arachnid that has the head and thorax.

chelicera (kih-LIH-suh-ruh) - either of the leglike organs of a spider that has a fang attached to it.

digestive - of or relating to the breakdown of food into substances small enough for the body to absorb.

family - a group that scientists use to classify similar plants or animals. It ranks above a genus and below an order.

inject - to forcefully introduce a fluid into the body, usually with a needle or something sharp.

migrate - to move from one place to another, often to find food.

nocturnal (nahk-TUHR-nuhl) - active at night.

pedipalp (PEH-duh-palp) - either of the leglike organs of a spider that are used to sense motion and catch prey.

predator - an animal that kills and eats other animals.

retreat - a place where an animal or a person goes to have privacy or safety.

spinneret - either of the two body parts attached to the abdomen of a spider where the silk is made.

venom - a poison produced by some animals and insects. It usually enters a victim through a bite or sting.

WEB SITES

To learn more about recluse spiders, visit ABDO Publishing Company on the World Wide Web at **www.abdopub.com**. Web sites about these spiders are featured on our Book Links page. These links are routinely monitored and updated to provide the most current information available.

INDEX